Science

Peter Shaw

Citation Press, New York 1972

This book is published simultaneously in Great
Britain, Canada and other countries of the British
Commonwealth by Macmillan Education Ltd and
in the United States by Citation Press, Library
and Trade Division, Scholastic Magazines, Inc.

Cover photograph by courtesy of Henry Grant

Designer Richard Hollis

Printed in the U.S.A.

Preface

The purpose of the Anglo-American Primary Education Project is to provide descriptions of the way that British primary schools work. They are published in this series of booklets under the general title of *Informal Schools in Britain Today* and they have been written for American and British educators and teachers-in-training as well as for the general public.

The authors are either practitioners or expert observers of British primary education and, in most cases, they document the work of the schools through detailed case examples; where it is relevant, implications are stated and conclusions drawn. It is not the intention to provide theoretical discussions or prescriptive manuals to informal education, but rather to present accounts from which deductions and generalizations can be made. In so doing, these booklets draw on the experience of that large minority of primary schools that have adopted informal methods.

It is hoped that the booklets will help educators who are looking for examples to substantiate change in particular schools and also those who are concerned, as teachers, educators or administrators, with the wider implications of the education of young children. For students who plan to become teachers these accounts of what happens in the classrooms of British primary schools provide ample material for discussion as well as helpful insights into the practice of teaching.

The series has been prepared under the aegis of the Schools Council in England with the support of the Ford Foundation in the United States. Planning was assisted by a small Anglo-American advisory group whose members are listed on page 4. The views expressed are however personal to each author.

British Directorate

Geoffrey Cockerill, Project Chairman/Joint Secretary, Schools Council for Curriculum and Examinations, London.

John Blackie/Formerly Chief Inspector, Primary Education, Department of Education and Science, London.

Molly Brearley/Formerly Principal, Froebel Institute College of Education, London.

Maurice Kogan, Project Co-ordinator/Professor of Government and Social Administration, School of Social Sciences, Brunel University, Uxbridge, Middlesex.

American Participants

J. Myron Atkin/Dean, School of Education, University of Illinois, Urbana, Illinois.

Ann Cook/Co-director, Community Resources Institute, 270 W. 96th Street, New York.

Joseph Featherstone/Writer; Lecturer, John Fitzgerald Kennedy School of Government, Institute of Politics, Harvard University, Cambridge, Massachusetts.

Professor David Hawkins/Director, Mountain View Center for Environmental Education, University of Colorado, Boulder, Colorado.

Herb Mack/Co-director, Community Resources Institute, 270 W. 96th Street, New York.

Marjorie Martus/Program Officer, The Ford Foundation, New York, N.Y.

Casey Murrow/Teacher, Wilmington Elementary School, Wilmington, Vermont.

Liza Murrow/Antioch-Putney Graduate School of Education, Putney, Vermont.

Mary Lela Sherburne/Director, Pilot Communities Project, Education Development Center, Newton, Mass.

4

Contents

The Author

Peter Shaw is principal lecturer in Natural Sciences at the Froebel Institute. He is interested in fostering an active, practical, and involved approach to the learning of science. He enjoys teaching through field work, in any branch of science, but especially in biology, particularly marine biology.

Mr Shaw's interests have been developed through both his work at the Froebel Institute and his activities for the Natural Science Society, of which he was exhibition secretary for several years. He now edits the Society's journal, NATURAL SCIENCE IN SCHOOLS.

1 What is Science ?

To many people the word science conjures up a picture of white-coated technicians carrying out experiments in a well-equipped laboratory. Films and television frequently foster this impression with views of flasks and other glassware, in which chemicals bubble merrily, or of banks of electronic apparatus. All too often the popular view of science is of a complicated activity, reserved for specially qualified and trained personnel.

Nothing could be further from the truth. Science should rather be seen as a way of looking at the environment and building up a store of information about it. Every individual continually explores his surroundings in a scientific way, whether he is aware of it or not.

Scientific investigation begins with observations, using human senses and technical aids, as each is appropriate. As more and more observational records are built up, it becomes possible to see relationships between separate events, to classify the information obtained, to begin to make generalizations, and to distinguish between 'usual' and 'unusual' observations. Many observations or sets of observations need to be explained. Basically, a scientific hypothesis is an intelligent guess at an explanation, based on all relevant information currently available. A hypothesis is not true just because it sounds convincing; it must be tested by further observations and by experiment. The ultimate test available to science is the *controlled experiment* where the results of one experiment are compared with those of another, identical in every respect except that of the one factor being tested. Even a series of experiments do not prove that a hypothesis always holds good. However, it becomes increasingly credible where it remains valid in the light of information discovered after it was propounded, and especially if it has been able to predict such information. Nevertheless, every hypothesis remains vulnerable to even a single observation or experimental result which appears to contradict it.

Throughout history, man has explored his environment. When sufficient observations were recorded, it became possible to organize the information. Although the idea of a controlled experiment is a comparatively recent one, attempts were made to explain, and despite new developments in technique, observations remain the basis of all scientific investigations.

Science as we know it today is an uncompleted jigsaw puzzle, the pieces (large and small) which have been put together being the work of countless observers and investigators. These workers have been united by the compulsion of human curiosity, a driving force which has spurred men to major practical and intellectual efforts in tackling their problems. Both the endeavours themselves and the possibility of making discoveries, have been a source of satisfaction to a large number of scientists. Discoveries of facts, or relationships, new to the individual involved, have frequently resulted in feelings of intense joy, and in almost child-like behaviour. The story of Archimedes' unattired eruption into the outside world is probably merely an exaggerated account of his actual delight.

Over all, science is best considered as a vast body of connected knowledge and, at the same time, as the relationship between this *expanding* knowledge and the method by which it has been obtained. Because so-called scientific 'facts' are always subject to further observations and to experimental test, the mass of knowledge is likely to continue to expand. Although the actual body of information is central to science and clearly important in its own right, it is the *method* which is so distinctive to science.

2 Science in the Primary School

Scientific development in children, like development in other fields, is progressive, and a very individual process. Thus any arbitrary distinction, such as that between various types of school (infant, junior, etc) is of limited value. It is important, too, not to limit consideration to the school situation, since the development of scientific knowledge and abilities begins long before a child reaches school age, and continues outside school hours.

In many ways, the development of scientific knowledge and abilities in children mirrors the historical evolution of scientific progress. At the earliest stage, observation, making use of all available senses, is almost the only aspect to be considered. As development proceeds, observations (and, later, second-hand information) will be analysed and classified, unusual features will be noted, and generalizations will be made. Some ideas will be tested both by questions to others and by further first-hand investigations. However, it is important to note that the idea of an experiment (and especially any concept of a controlled experiment) is rather subtle, and may not necessarily be discovered by any particular individual. Certainly one must not *expect* primary school children to engage in sophisticated experiments, although many children will see the need for 'fairness' in their investigations.

In the light of the above remarks it is illuminating to attempt to list some of the *working assumptions* (either stated or merely implied) which are made by 'progressive' educators in science;

ie, those who build up the learning framework from studies of the child and his behaviour.

These suggest that:

1. a child is very interested in his environment;

2. observation is the primary way of increasing understanding of the world;

3. related observations are progressively linked together to give greater understanding;

4. attempts to assimilate information give rise to problems—a child may want (indeed *need*) to know the answers to these, and an intense learning force may be provoked;

5. as it is impossible to predict which experiences will provoke interest and encourage observations in any particular child at any specific time, a wide variety of stimuli (provision) is necessary;

6. children have a need (and often a desire) to communicate the results of their observations, and the ideas which develop from them;

7. free discussion (both with other children and with adults) aids understanding, and provides a stimulus for further enquiry;

8. problems are best tackled by practical investigation;

9. the most effective learning is obtained when children's investigations are aided, rather than directed, by the teacher;

10. second-hand information is of greatest value when it can be integrated with recently acquired (or possibly, recently considered) first-hand experiences;

11. although the *integrated* body of knowledge built up by a child is important, it is not necessary (at the pre-secondary stage at least) to define which particular pieces of scientific information should be acquired, although some *concepts* may be considered necessary. There are many topics in which children are very likely to be interested.

However important science may be, it is only part of the learning process. Nevertheless, the enthusiasm generated in the course of an active first-hand investigation of the environment can be relied upon to provide stimulus for other aspects of learning, including the traditional 'three Rs'. (The relationship of these to science learning is shown in the diagram below.)

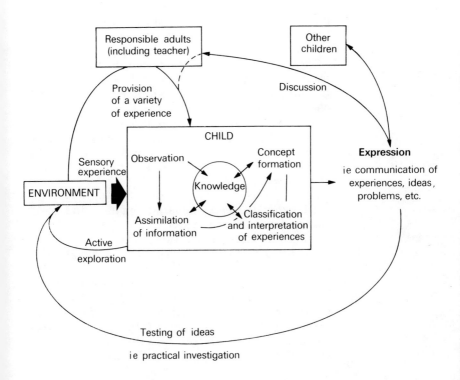

The techniques used to communicate experiences may be extremely varied. At the earliest stages of development, verbal expression will be of tremendous importance and may indeed remain dominant, at least for certain periods, later on. As other methods are seen to be of value they, too, are utilized. The *need* to communicate experiences gives meaning to writing, counting, etc, and provides some of the stimuli for expression in art, movement, music, and so on. Similarly, enthusiasm for finding out provides a strong motive to widen experience through the use of books and other written material. Thus the basic skills can be seen to be relevant to the process of living.

It is important to emphasize that the knowledge possessed by a child at a particular time (like human knowledge of science as a whole) will be incomplete and often inaccurate in parts. An active, practical approach to learning, however, will ensure that 'facts' are put to the test as necessary, and that ideas are progressively clarified.

Science is an important item in the 'curriculum' for young children, providing opportunities for learning which are co-ordinated within the child himself, yet arise from an almost endless list of possible interests. Paradoxically enough, this is perhaps best illustrated by indicating broad sequences of experience in comparatively limited fields of study. The topics will be considered under the following headings:

Invertebrate animals (small animals found under stones, logs, and in the soil)
Discarded materials (ie, 'rubbish')
Water

These areas have been selected because all or most of them provide material stimulus in the environment of every child. Thus they almost inevitably give rise to scientific interests (physical, chemical, and geological, as well as biological) for each child who engages in practical study of his local environment. Each of these topics, alone, opens up vast fields, and the examples given are but a minute fraction of the possible developments of the studies. The 'knowledge' component of the educative process, like that of science itself, is almost limitless, and no one individual can hope to amass more than a fraction of the total.

For convenience the examples quoted here (which are taken from several schools) have been assigned to age ranges as follows: pre-school, 0–5 years old; infant, 5–7 years old; young junior, 7–9 years old; and older junior, 9–11 years old.

Invertebrate animals
Small invertebrate animals ('creepy crawlies') found in the soil and under stones are often of great fascination to young children. On the other hand, these creatures are often abhorrent to adults and, not infrequently, their distaste, even when not openly expressed, is noted and sometimes imitated by children. Thus, this is a field in which it may be difficult for a teacher or other adult to become enthusiastic or even to permit exploration.

Pre-school experience
Caroline's first known contact with a worm was at the age of nine months. Exploration was brief but intense and involved mainly the senses of sight and touch but was brought to an end when she placed the worm in her mouth! During the next year or so she came across many other animals. Often, earlier experiences seemed to have been forgotten and questions were frequently repeated but new facts were discovered and formulated.

What's dat? . . . It's a worm. Worm . . . wriggle. . . . Touch a worm . . . 'nother worm . . . wriggle.

One result of this experience was the, probably accidental, making of a plasticine worm, though the interest in this was short-lived. However, the experience was not completely forgotten, even though it was four months before the next worm was discovered and by then the word 'worms' could not be recalled. After hearing them named and before touching the worms now found, Caroline said:

What do we do with worms? . . . We could kiss worms. One worm, two worms, three worms . . . lots of worms. Big worm . . . baby worm. Worm live in the ground.

She was then willing to handle the worms, making no attempt to put them in her mouth, but jumped away quickly when she believed she was standing on one, and was relieved to find that it was only a piece of plastic tube. The tube was examined at length, but there was unfortunately no verbal expression of the way in which it differed from a worm.

At about this time, many objects, animate and inanimate, were being explored. Slugs, snails and woodlice were found, and a group of ladybirds was discovered among some leaves. Pebbles had been collected, the variety of shape and size noted, and preference expressed for rounded ones. During general exploration on waste ground, a tiny spherical object was discovered: 'A lovely stone'.

Then the object unfolded itself in the warm palm of her hand to reveal itself as a pill woodlouse. The horror on her face, not expressed in words, was due not to the fact that something was crawling on her hand, but to the fact that the *stone* was crawling. Attempts to discuss this with her produced the eventual reply, 'We want to play ball now.'

After a gap of a few days, the search for stones was resumed. Presumably this was now a period when ideas about living and non-living things were being reappraised and new concepts formed. No further pill bugs were found, but about a week later a snail was described as a 'stone with a little animal in it', and a few weeks later, when a broken snail shell was found Caroline said, 'It's an egg cup . . . no, it's the skin off a snail. It's a bit like a petal' (a piece of apple blossom was picked up for comparison).

Of course, these experiences with snails and woodlice are but a fragment of the child's total experience at this stage, and much sorting out of information and progressive reclassifying is required as new information comes to hand. This record of Caroline's responses when attempting to name coloured pictures of birds illustrates this point:

. . . *pigeon* . . . *pigeon* . . . *dicky-bird* . . . *quacker-duck* (correct!) . . . *canary bird* (a yellow bird) . . . *ladybird*.

Starting school

Interest in small animals does not cease when a child begins school. Adrian was a shy youngster, having attended afternoon school for nearly five weeks without saying a single word in class. The class was asked to find animals and bring them to school. At home, Adrian insisted on searching waste ground with his mother, and (somewhat to her—hidden—horror) decided to take a large spider. He selected this creature specifically because of its impressive size and shape, and took it along to school in a container. His excited words, shouted as he entered the classroom, expressed the uninhibited pleasure of discovery: 'I gotta spider . . . I gotta *big* spider.'

He was then prepared to talk to the class in some detail about his find. There were many results from the number of animals brought into the classroom that afternoon, including naming, drawing, painting, counting, and model making. Probably none was more important than the development of Adrian's self-confidence.

An infant class

Young infants become progressively more ready to search carefully, examine in detail, and relate their findings to other experiences. A class searching in soil found a variety of creatures, and wanted to take them back and keep them in the classroom. Their interest and involvement is shown by some of the comments, writings and illustrations.

About a snail: 'It's got no feet.' 'It's like a slug with a shell.' 'There's a sticky mess behind it.' 'You can't pull it off.' 'A worm goes faster.' After watching the snail inside a glass jar: 'It's got its mouth in a funny place.' 'Sometimes snails climb over each other.'

More detailed examination followed, and Janet, having looked with the aid of a large magnifying-glass, told Angela that the things at the front were feelers: 'They've got blobs at the end.'

Angela was fascinated by the word 'feelers' and repeated it several times, trying to imitate their movement with her hands and body. Janet told her that there were eyes at the end of the feelers. She replied, 'They can't be eyes . . . they poke in when I touch them.'

John became fascinated by the empty snail shells he found. He brought several back to the classroom, commenting that they were to be homes for slugs. He ignored protests, from several children, that slugs didn't have shells, and put his collection with some slugs, examining them every day. He was delighted on the one occasion when he found a tiny slug right inside a large shell, and he drew it and wrote about it. He was quite undeterred by comments from his classmates that the shell was much too large.

The physical problems of housing the various animal finds had been discussed by the class as a whole. Suggestions for dealing with a snail were readily forthcoming. 'Put it in a big jar.' 'With leaves to keep it warm.'

Several children insisted that more than one snail should be put in a container, so that they wouldn't be lonely, and one suggested that they ought to have 'a mummy and a daddy snail', an idea which these children did not follow up. In helping the children to set up their vivaria the teacher, without comment, added the necessary moist earth and some stones. Several of the children insisted that holes should be pierced in the lid so that the snails could breathe: 'Not too big or they will escape.'

A request for information about the food of snails produced a multitude of ideas ranging from 'dirt' (this child was probably thinking of worms) to a very specific suggestion: 'My daddy doesn't like snails. They eat lettuce.' Lettuce was brought to school that afternoon, and then daily!

Throughout their explorations and discussions the children were obviously concerned for the animals' welfare, which they related to their own well-being. No mention was made by the teacher of the necessity for moisture (or even for water to drink). However, they were quick to notice the behaviour of the snails in drier conditions. At first the suggestion was that the creatures were asleep but it was noted that: 'They come out when you hold them upside down.'

Suggestions were made regarding ways of making the animals more active.

'Make the holes bigger.' 'He doesn't need more food. He likes lettuce.' 'Put some *proper* soil in.'

This last suggestion came after the soil in the vivarium had been felt; the idea was followed up. When the snails were later seen to be more active, comments were made. One was particularly perceptive: 'He likes it better. It's more like outside.'

At the time this work was being carried out, a snail was being featured in a daily series of animated puppet films on television. Remarks from the children showed that watching these cartoons had probably enabled them to note more readily some structural features of the snails they found. However, the picture on the television screen may well have given rise to some confusion about the size of animals (at least two children were surprised by the 'small size' of quite large garden snails) and about the conditions in which they lived. It is interesting that no one suggested naming the snails found (possibly because there were so many other animals in the classroom at the time), so that the name of the television puppet was not mentioned.

A young junior group

A group of lower juniors were able to take their studies further. Many quite casual observations were recorded in detail: 'The noise of the aeroplanes does not frighten the snails.'

More detail of structure was seen: 'The snail has little feelers and big feelers.' 'A snail has a moth (mouth) with two lips. Its skin is slimy.' 'He has a breathing hole. It closes when it goes in his shell.'

While watching a snail eat flour, spread inside a jam-jar: 'It chews its food.'

Several lines of investigation into the behaviour of snails were followed. In the course of measuring how far snails moved, one child suggested putting one into the middle of the playground.

Andrew did not approve of the idea: 'He'd never get to the side. It would be like a million miles to him.'

Actual measurements were made, and records were kept for specific animals: 'The green snail walked one foot in 3 minutes 25 seconds.'

When commenting on the speeds recorded for snails of different sizes James wrote: 'We think that size does not have anything to do with the snail's speed and movement.'

Work developed to investigations of the progress of snails over various surfaces: 'It took longest on foam and ruff (rough) wood.' 'On the foam all the slime soaked in.'

Problems arose which needed to be solved or, sometimes, simply accepted—animals did not always move in the required direction! Snail tracks were drawn—and these stimulated pictures and finger paintings. Sometimes snails became inactive during the course of a test: 'In my picture I have done two snails awake and two snails asleep.'

The noise of the
aeroplanes dose not
frighten the snails.

However, when snails were active, their movements could be examined in minute detail: 'Under the snail there is lots of little lines . . . they move up when the snail moves.'

When snails moved vertically instead of horizontally, their progress was timed; gravity did not seem to restrict their movements!

Alongside of this, studies of the many other invertebrates found were being developed. Life cycles were studied, including that of a pupa which later emerged as a moth. Much basic observational work was carried out and recorded, and details of structure and function were checked by reference to books. This in turn led to further investigations; the statement that woodlice lived in dark damp places led to tests to find out the conditions preferred by woodlice, and the results were set out in the form of block graphs and as 'sets'.

Investigations of the preference of invertebrate animals for moist places were further stimulated by the discovery of escapees from vivaria. Some of these had become stranded on the floor of the classroom and had become dry and brittle.

A group of older juniors

A group of older juniors became involved in invertebrate studies when, at playtime, they found slugs, woodlice, and a worm, under a felt sheet left, following building work, in the corner of the playground. A thorough search indicated that the same animals did not seem to be present in other places, although spiders had been observed (but not collected) behind a drain pipe.

Encouraged by the teacher, the children recorded information about the animals and where they had been discovered, and drew a large plan of the playground to show exactly where they had made their find. Asked why they thought the animals were there, they put forward plenty of suggestions: 'They came with the sheet.' 'Because it's dark there.' 'It's wet too.' 'The animals are safe from birds.'

They eagerly responded to the suggestion that they should put out another piece of sheeting to see if animals came under that one, and they examined the sheet daily. After heavy rain one night, they noticed that the water remained longer under the sheet than elsewhere. 'It's wet now, there *should* be worms here.' 'Perhaps they haven't found it yet.'

The school caretaker threw away the felt sheet after four days! Although, later on, the children put down more pieces, and were eventually rewarded by finding life under some of them, they did not, at the time the experiment took place, continue to question *how* the animals had arrived there.

In the meantime, tests were devised to find out whether the animals were seeking darkness or wetness. The apparatus was basically simple, consisting of a transparent plastic container with a lid. To subject the animals to wet and dry conditions the floor of the container was covered, half with moist and half with dry blotting paper. Technical problems had to be tackled, as when, for example, water crept along the blotting paper from the moist half to the dry. This difficulty was eventually overcome by using two smaller pieces of paper, with a gap between them, and dampening one. A dark/light chamber was made, merely by covering one half of the plastic box with dark paper.

Woodlice showed a marked preference for damp conditions. The group concerned were so delighted by establishing this that they demonstrated their tests to all comers, almost as a party trick! The dark/light tests were not so convincing but, consequently, the children were ready to record results, repeat tests, and set out answers graphically. One girl concluded: 'We think the woodlice are happier when it is dark.'

When housing animals, the children were again ready to tackle practical problems as they arose, and seemed aware of the sort of conditions in which the animals would survive. Similarly, they were able to anticipate the results of searching for further specimens: 'There will be more in the wood' (a patch of scrub near the school).

Not only were more animals found, but so was a greater range of material, and this extended the interest to many other children in the class.

Animals were examined in detail, and intensive use was made of books. An elaborate scheme of grouping animals was built up, based on resemblances and differences, and approaching a real zoological classification. Some animals, such as the centipede, presented problems—it was not easy to count its legs: 'It's a centipede. That means it's got a hundred legs.'

Later (with difficulty) the legs were counted on a centipede, found dead. The number was checked and agreed.

Another older-junior group

Another group of older juniors became involved in similar investigations after being shown a film strip on 'Waste Ground'. Some interesting problems developed. Stephen commented that nobody had found woodlice anywhere except huddled under stones and solid debris: 'They *must* eat sometime.'

He decided that this must happen at night, and

he worked out that a jar sunk in the ground might 'catch woodlice when they are out hunting.' He probably got this idea from reading about pitfall traps used for capturing larger animals. He covered the top of the jar with a few strands of fine grass: 'If it's dark they won't be able to see much.'

After nothing was captured on the first night, he put out other traps just to make sure. He kept careful records and displayed them to the class. At the end of each day he remembered to check his traps to make sure that no animals had fallen into them during the day. Although few animals were caught in his traps he concluded to his satisfaction that 'woodlice hunt at night.'

However, there was one unexpected observation; the presence in one of the jars, of a centipede eating a small worm. Other children were fascinated by this, and several agreed to try to find out what their animals ate. At first, tests were crude, but refinements were evolved during 'discussion'. For example, children worked out that the animals might have gone towards some food items not because these were preferred, but because they were nearer or larger. In the case of some animals, for example, slugs, the children found it easy to see which foods had been 'nibbled' and could even examine 'teeth marks', but the results were very confused, as preferences seemed to change without apparent reason.

Stephen got nowhere with his tests on woodlice, and eventually concluded: 'Woodlice did not seem to have a preference for anything we gave them. I think they just like soil.'

Linda, in attempting to find out how fast woodlice move, discovered that they were more willing to run when put out on an open floor. At first, she had tried to channel them down a straight run made from strips of cardboard but found that they 'pile up on top of one another and creep into every corner'. She solved her problem by letting each animal loose on a large piece of paper and making a track behind it with a fibre-tip pen. She had intended to snake string over each mark and then measure the string. However, someone in the class had shown her how to use a Meccano wheel as what was described as a 'mini' trundle wheel (the class had made quite extensive use of a trundle wheel in work in mathematics). It is interesting, however, that Linda merely recorded her measurements in *turns* (of the wheel) and was only able to translate these into standard units following a group discussion. Needless to say, the 'mini' trundle found many other practical uses.

Colin, when searching waste ground, spent some time examining daisy heads. He later confessed disappointment that he had not found any earwigs on them. He had remembered one rather vivid close-up picture in the film strip, depicting an earwig on a daisy head, and believed that daisies were the usual habitat of earwigs!

Discarded materials

Man seems to be an animal whose production of rubbish is for ever ahead of his ability to dispose of it adequately. Some litter is, of course, unpleasant to handle, or even dangerous, but a substantial quantity of the discarded material which, unfortunately, forms part of our environment, is safe, solid, relatively clean, and often almost indestructable. This material can be of tremendous fascination to children and may stimulate work leading to quite complex mathematics as well as to physical and chemical investigations.

An infant class

Some response seems inevitable when such material is found or displayed on an infant-class interest table. The initial reaction, 'It's all dirty', gives way to intense interest as sorting proceeds: 'This is heavy.' 'The tin is rusty . . . it crumbles in my hands.'

One group spent a lot of time sorting out and naming and classifying a whole variety of materials including metal, plastic, rubber, leather, wood, etc. Various criteria were used in grouping, including size, shape, texture and colour, and the results were charted. Not infrequently there were discussions regarding the correct category for specific items, and sometimes this necessitated the creation of new groups.

Two children became quite absorbed in pieces of china, and brought along many fragments of that material. This resulted in strenuous efforts to piece it together and to assess exactly what each fragment represented. In addition, intricate details of pattern, glazing, etc, were commented upon and discussed. In fact, these children were getting the real feeling of being archaeologists, an impression which would have been reinforced, if they had been older, by the discovery of a large piece of a King George VI coronation mug!

A frequent response to scrap material, by infant children, is to use it for model making. Mark used a length of pipe, gauze, and various pieces of plastic and wood to construct his moon rocket. The string of verbal comments as he worked, and his later illustrations, indicated his plans for the journeys which his rocket would make. However, the actual construction, and the comment he wrote to accompany the displayed model, showed concern with more down-to-earth relationships. A metal bottle top attached to the side of the rocket was described as the steering wheel, and Mark wrote: 'My rocket is going to the moon. My rocket is ten inches high.'

Jane was fascinated by the fact that the world looked red through a piece of red plastic sheet which she discovered. She was able to relate this to the colours visible through pieces of cellophane provided by the teacher; she made more precise observations of apparent changes in colour which occurred when different objects were viewed, and of different effects obtained when looking through two differently coloured pieces of cellophane. Her interest declined in the face of difficulties she encountered when trying to make particular colours with powder paints.

Metals provoked a variety of activities. Alan

insisted, 'Metals go rusty. They go rusty when they get wet.' Further sorting threw doubts on this and, after discussion, various pieces of metal were left outside in a polythene-lined box. The children were, however, more fascinated by the method they developed for making records than by analysing results in any detail. The accidental discovery of the fact that damp rust would rub off on to paper focused attention on this as a technique of recording results pictorially as well as verbally. Other activities did, however, develop further. The provision of a small but powerful magnet gave impetus to a new kind of sorting and classifying: 'All the rusty things are picked up.' 'Even the crumbly bits of rust stuck to my magnet.'

When one of the boys brought a larger magnet, comparisons were provoked: 'Pins *leap* up to this magnet.' 'They jump much further than to the little one.'

Extensive pictorial lists, of what things were and what things were not attracted by their magnets, were drawn up, and attempts were made to weigh and measure some of the larger objects lifted.

An interest in sound (musical sounds) developed as a result of testing the noise made by some of the objects found. Objects were tapped, scraped, shaken, and knocked together. A lot of interest was focused on a seemingly unopenable tin, and guesses were made as to the contents. The caretaker's wrench eventually revealed the contents as coarse gravel. One development of this discovery was the making of various musical 'shakers', using tins and rigid plastic pots as containers. In selecting contents for their instruments, the children were clearly mindful of the possibilities presented by the scrap materials they had found, and stone, sand, plastic beads, and pieces of metal were all utilized. In many cases the children attempted to forecast the sort of sound which would be made. Many of the children could make correct use of the terms 'high' and 'low' in describing the notes they produced.

Other children tried to make musical notes by

scraping and rubbing. Pamela brought to school a flat tin with elastic bands stretched across it. While she was demonstrating it, she found that it made much more noise when placed on a table than on a padded surface. An immediate explanation was forthcoming: 'The foam is a bit pinchety' (her word) 'and it stops the noise getting down.'

Further investigations were put in hand, and the volume of sound produced on various surfaces was assessed and compared. Pamela was then prepared to generalize as a result of her studies: 'The foam is soft to keep our feet warm but the floor is hard so it plays better on the floor.'

Artistic techniques were frequently used by the children to communicate information. Rubbing, done earlier by some of the class, was used as a way of listing some of the materials discovered. Shoe soles, window panes, a strawberry net, wallpaper, a sieve, and a loudspeaker grill were among the objects of which rubbings were made. The use of rust marks smeared on paper was extended, from mere recording, to a way of making pictures. Gear wheels were used both for printing and for rolling out patterns (the latter technique has since been developed commercially). Sometimes art and science were, almost literally, blended together. Materials found were sorted according to their suitability for grinding into powders, and the children readily responded to the suggestion that they might mix these with water and use them in their painting.

A backward infant group

A group òf older (but below average ability) infants was able to extend some of the scientific investigations further (although their spelling left something to be desired!). Here are some of their practical responses to ideas put forward by the teacher:

'I think any metal sticks to magnets.' 'I thound out theat sum metals stick beta thean uvas.' 'I tooc a magnet and sor how meny nails I could get in a row 5.' 'I sor how meny nails I could get on a magnet.

111.' 'Magnets stil[stick] froo warta and glars and cardbord and me.' 'I ferst took sum bottels and filld eech one with a diffarant amount of water. Then I sor how meny diffarnt sounds I could mace. The les warta in it the hiya note I got.' 'I took a bottle and bloo across top. It made a thuny sound. Then I thild it with water it made no sound.'

. Magnets stil froo warta, and glars and card bord and me.

A backward older-junior child

With juniors, many further developments are possible, although many children, and probably especially those who have had little previous experience in this particular field, need to go through some of the earlier stages. For example, the book of rubbings produced by this older junior was to him as essential a part of the recording process as it was to an infant.

Often backward children get their important stimulus for effort from practical exploration. Charlie (aged ten) had been in trouble with authority (including the police) during his three years in the junior school and was barely literate. One of his pleasures was to be allowed to go with a relation to deliver coal, on some Saturday mornings. Perhaps his most sustained piece of work arose through finding pieces of coal and coke on a rubbish dump. Patiently he became involved, at times with a school friend (his only one, and intermittent at that), in crushing up coal for a model coal truck; in drawing, using coal and coke; in naming fuels from samples and illustrations obtained (by the teacher) from a coal merchant; and in building a model coal mine, using balsa wood, corrugated paper, and some of his crushed coal. This work may not sound impressive, but it involved him for lengthy periods, and he was willing to turn to simple reference books, especially to the pictures in them, for guidance. Some of his work was recorded in written form.

Later he began (as he put it) to 'find which coal is the heaviest' by weighing samples on the scales, but he was distracted from this by (rare) involvement with another group who provided him with a meccano lift to go with his coal mine. Other members of the group tried to test the hardness of some coal, using a hand drill, but this interest was, unfortunately, not developed.

An older-junior group
Able juniors are, of course, capable of much further progress in their physical studies, leading to quite advanced concepts. The response of one group to a rusty bicycle wheel, still in its frame, indicates the variety of stimuli which may arise.

'It's all rusty.' 'Not all; it's still shiny where there's chromium plating.' 'You can twang the spokes. It's like a harp.' 'There aren't many different notes, though.' (This interest was later followed up with wheels and individual spokes of different sizes.) 'It's like a spinning wheel.' 'It's stuck; it won't move.' 'It needs oiling.'

After the wheel had been oiled and eased: 'It takes nothing at all to turn it.' The ease with which the wheel moved when a very small piece of plasticine was stuck on, demonstrated this: 'It's a balance. We could use it for scales.' Several children followed this up and, with weights hooked on to the spokes, the sensitivity of the balance was assessed and compared with that of other scales in the classroom. So concerned were these children with solving technical problems and making their apparatus as efficient as possible, that many of the scientific possibilities of their investigation were overlooked.

Tests on rusting did lead to further work, beginning with detailed records showing which items rusted and exactly where rust was found on pieces of scrap. Tests were worked out to discover the influence of paint and chromium plating on rusting, and the effects of oil in preventing deterioration. Comparison of the effects of moisture on different substances revealed metallic changes other than rusting, and initiated practical studies of moulds. A textbook suggestion for demonstrating the need for air in the rusting process was attempted, but the absence of a clear-cut result reduced faith in this line of investigation.

An older-junior class

A completely different class, given very similar starting points, were able to exploit the mathematical possibilities of their physical observations more fully. Studies developed to include measurements of the actual force required to turn a bicycle wheel, using both weights and a spring balance; and the differing forces required at various distances from the centre of the wheel were not only noted but also recorded and graphed. This, in turn, led to an appreciation of the relationship between the circumference and diameter of various wheels, and of the use of linked wheels and of gear wheels in transmitting movement. Measurements were also made of the forces involved in putting on brakes and, in the event of brake failure, of the effects of crashes occurring on slopes of varying degrees of steepness.

Though these children did not neglect the possibilities for imaginative use of the material at their disposal, their 'inventions' showed appreciation of the real physical relationships between individual components.

Other members of the same class became involved in quite different topics. Many of the substances found were closely examined, and use was made of aids for magnification. For example, in assessment of the size of the threads in cloth-like materials, human hairs were used for comparison with the finer strands. After discussion, crude apparatus to compare and measure strengths was designed. Although their 'experiments' did not meet the rigorous standards of true science, the children were concerned to compare like with like, and realized the limitations of their results. Clearly, too, they were able to see their results in terms of the graphs constructed, and to use these mathematical displays to read and predict results.

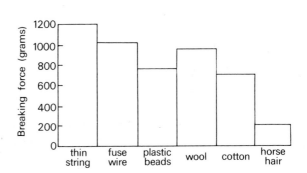

The fascination of these practical tests helped to encourage other practical work concerning, for example, the amount of stretching which could take place in different materials.

Another line of study developed into an investigation of the degree of slide (ie, absence of friction) produced by the soles of various items of footwear. A spring balance was used to measure the force needed to make a shoe move on each surface tested. Comparisons were made, both using the same soles on different surfaces and using different soles on the same surface. The work not only gave an appreciation of the nature and physical properties of a variety of different substances but also enabled numerical comparisons to be made, such as those shown in the following graph.

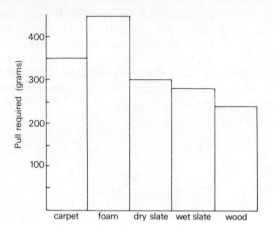

The force required
to move a shoe on
various surfaces

Another older-junior class

It is interesting to set these studies alongside of similar work followed through in another quite different class. Some of the children had commented on the increased strength of fibres when these were woven. (Initially, exploration had arisen from suggestions made by the teacher in connexion with observations of silk moths spinning cocoons.) Silk and nylon, in strand and woven form, were compared, using simple breaking tests.

At this time, David found some sodden paper sacks, and was surprised by how easily they could be torn; he had believed that they were waterproof and strong. He readily agreed to use the material test rig to compare samples, and he was most insistent on using pieces of exactly the same size in his experiments. The tests were repeated several times, but he was disappointed that the paper often tore at the point where it was attached. He improved the apparatus by adding rubbers between the pieces of ruler previously used for holding the paper, and demonstrated to his satisfaction that the wet paper was considerably less strong than the dry. (See the diagram opposite.)

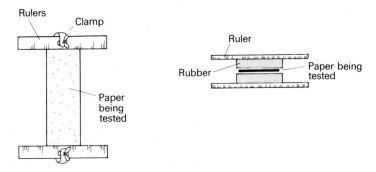

Apparatus to test the strength of paper: (a) top view of clamping arrangements, (b) side view

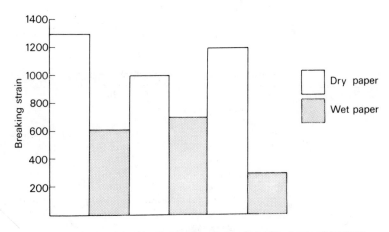

Graph to show the breaking strains of samples of wet and dry paper

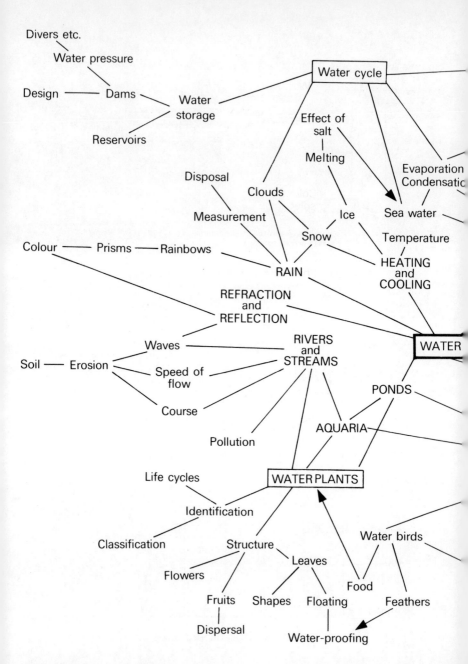

34

Water works

Crystals

Water in food   Water in living organisms

Filtration

Coloured drinks

Dyes

Coloured solutions   Chemical reactions

DISSOLVING

Rusting etc.

Boats ——— Plimsol line

Displacement

SINKING and FLOATING   Density

Speed ——————— Streamlining

Swimming   Strokes

Dissolving of gases   Swimming baths — Capacity

Gills   Movement

WATER ANIMALS   Shape

Fish ——— Structure ——— "Dissection"

Small invertebrates   Economic uses

Life cycles   Fishing

Identification (use of lenses etc.)

Movement   Strength of fishing lines

Feet   Classification

Discussion with the teacher, and with a group, brought up the suggestion that sacks might be improved, and also produced ideas for carrying out and testing such modifications. Although many minds contributed suggestions, David was responsible for the practical work of trying out the effects of fat, oil, polish, and model aircraft 'dope' on the properties of the paper. He tried to assess whether water had been absorbed by a particular piece of paper by balancing it against another one of identical size.

Water   As water seems to have an irresistible attraction for children, it is perhaps fitting to use it in an example of the range of studies which may arise as a result of practical exploration of the surroundings. The flow diagram is often used by teachers to anticipate work which may arise as a result of environmental investigations—although a teacher must be prepared for the probability that some of his expectations will not be fulfilled, and that young minds may react with quite novel ideas and interests. The same technique for indicating radiating, and sometimes interlinked, sequences of work, may be utilized for summarizing events which have occurred in a single class.

The flow diagram shown on pages 34–5 incorporates the results of observations made in many junior school classes. It is still not complete, and only work in science is shown, because the range of activities is far greater than the space available in which to record them. It would be illuminating for the reader to try to extend the list of possibilities, or to develop the possibilities which arise when topics which have arisen are put at the centre of a new flow diagram. Many of the topics listed can engage (and *have* engaged) the study of infants and, indeed, even of pre-school children.

The extent to which work can develop may be illustrated by taking just two examples from this extensive range.

1. Pond life Fishing for animal life in ponds, ditches and streams seems to have an attraction for children from a very early age. The interest may be only short-lived, and often consist of no more than catching, and either releasing or attempting to keep, tadpoles, sticklebacks, etc. This comparatively superficial approach may persist but such interests, whether present or initiated, can be developed to encourage much more detailed studies.

2. Moving water Moving water seems to have a greater attraction than still water, for all age groups, and, when the opportunity presents itself, the youngest children will make use of moving water in their play. A fascinating example is 'Pooh sticks', the game described by A. A. Milne in *Winnie-the-Pooh*. (The game consists of dropping sticks into a stream on the upstream side of a bridge, and seeing which stick first appears on the downstream side.)

Children may indeed make their first discovery of the fact that streams are in motion by observing objects floating on the surface (although other explanations are also put forward).

A class of older juniors, familiar with the above story, but of limited ability (and not renowned for their application to 'conventional' school work in general or mathematics in particular) were persuaded to measure, and later to graph, the speed of water flow in a local stream. Even before they made any measurements, they met and reported upon various problems—the presence of 'whirlpools' in the stream, places where the flow of water always carried objects to the side, and so on. Sticks did not always travel at the same speed, and particularly when they were irregularly shaped, got stuck, while pieces of polystyrene were blown to the edge. The children suggested the use of petals (although they were only partly able to express the advantage of these in being small, light, and reasonably waterproof), and it was their idea, too, to release the petals in a particular colour sequence, in order to in my drop of water they were two animals one of them is long and thin and it is yellow it keeps twisting and turning they is three strands on the tail end and it has two feelers and it has no legs when it was placed under a magnifying projector we saw it had two eyes and two suckers. and it was a Midge Larva

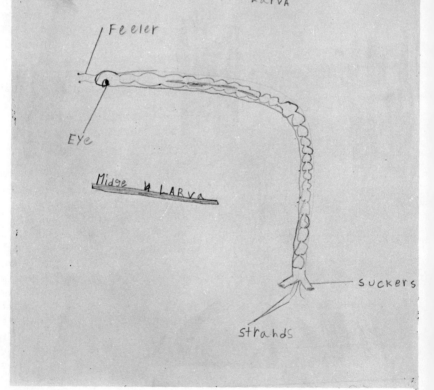

Feeler

Eye

Midge LARVA

suckers

strands

'Midge Larva'

My Observations

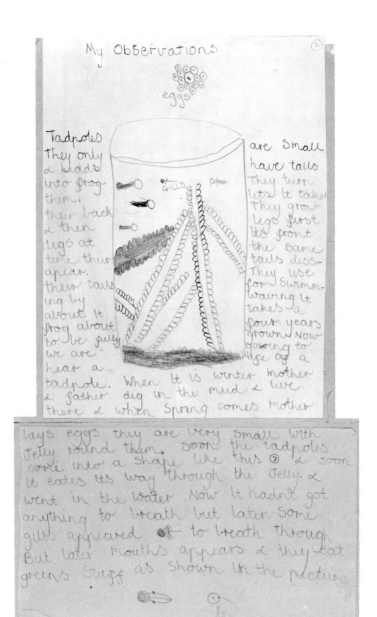

eggs

Tadpoles are small They only have tails a heads They turn into frog- lets it takes them. They grow their back legs first a then its front legs at the same time their tails dis- apear. They use their tails for swimm- ing by waving It about It takes a frog about four years to be fully grown Now we are going to hear a age of a tadpole. When It is winter mother a father dig in the mud a live. there a when spring comes mother

lays eggs they are very small with jelly round them. Soon the tadpoles come into a shape like this ⊙ a soon It eates its way through the jelly a went in the water Now It hadn't got anything to breath but later some gills appeared to breath through. But later mouths appears a they eat greens stuff as shown in the picture

'My observations'

make it easier to follow their progress.

Perhaps more important than the work achieved was their attitude. As one remarked to a visitor: 'She don't know it's our 'obby.' Not only was 'she' (the teacher) fully aware of their interest but she was aware that they did not realize the extent of her knowledge! Thus, when at the end of the week she remarked to them; 'I wonder whether the rain will make the stream flow faster on Saturday', they did not guess that they were being 'set' weekend homework. Not only did they 'do' this homework but they came back asking how they could measure how much rain had fallen.

3 Conclusion

These examples, taken together, raise many interesting points. From the amount of enthusiasm generated, and energy harnessed, it seems evident that a study of the environment[1] in practical terms is so important that we cannot afford to neglect it. A scientific approach, being basically a method which helps an individual to retain his innate curiosity, and to use his developing intellectual powers in conjunction with this important characteristic, is surely one relevant to all human beings and not just to future scientists. The variety of topics available for study is so vast that it is hardly surprising that many people might wish to limit the amount taught. Certainly the individual has to limit his intake, but is it not perhaps *too* convenient to suggest that it should be limited *for him*, as is done by some restricted syllabuses? In some such cases it is all too easy for learning to take place without the necessity for individual thought. The willingness of human beings to learn is certainly not confined to accepted school subjects, and may often be greater in 'non-academic' pursuits.

The children mentioned in the examples above had to think for themselves and, usually, to communicate with others. Although help was always available to them, they were often prepared to accept the challenge offered by the problems in hand, and to seek solutions by trial and error, through discussion and from books, as well as by the seemingly simpler technique of 'asking the teacher'. They knew that the results of many of the investigations depended entirely on them, and in this situation the fact that some experiments didn't 'work properly' or produce the 'right' answer was

[1]See, in this series,
ENVIRONMENTAL
STUDIES by
Melville Harris

41

of less importance than it might have been in a more formal situation. Unexpected results frequently provoked further interest, and failures of tests gave an excuse for repetition of observation—often very necessary if techniques are to be learned and information assimilated. Within the limited field each child studied, he became an 'expert', with the knowledge gained being relevant and connected.

In nearly all of the examples described, the activities were largely carried out by groups of children, rather than by the whole class, although discussions, and other methods of sharing experiences, by displays, etc, brought together larger numbers of children. Thus, at a particular instant of time there was a variety of work taking place within each classroom, not all of it necessarily either scientific or practical. Working in this way it is not possible, at the beginning of any particular term or year, to predict what scientific knowledge any child will gain (is it ever possible?). Consequently, conventional examinations are not practicable—in some fields a child would know more than the teacher setting the test! Much more reliance has therefore to be placed on the teacher's continuous records and over-all assessment.

This dependence on subjective criteria has advantages, as children cannot be graded merely on numerical evidence. The depth of involvement of the children in their activities is some measure of their achievement, as is the degree to which they themselves raise further problems for observation and investigation. Although written work may be assessed, it becomes essential to take into account other methods of communication, including the spoken word. Thus, evaluation of each child's progress is, of necessity, on a broad front.

Although the specific topics described above did arise in the classes mentioned, they need not have done. Even similar stimuli produced different responses in apparently similar classes, and variations in individual interests, in environment, and between teachers, ensure that each child will see different starting points. In general, it is probably true to say that the younger or less experienced the child, the more local his interests—which, as he develops, will expand geographically as well as intellectually. For this reason alone, the possibility that work already 'covered' at an earlier age may be repeated need not be of particular concern.

When what is to be presented is left so open, it is important to note that certain aspects are unsuitable at a particular stage. For example, it would not be possible for a child to have an appreciation of density and of, say, Archimedes' principle until he had grasped the concepts of both weight and volume, and a fair amount of practical experience is required before even this is achieved.

The examples considered show considerable variations in the ability of children to express themselves and, to be more specific, standards of grammar and of spelling may differ from what might be desired. Such variations are, of course, to be expected, and the development of scientific abilities does not, of itself, aid progress in the basic skills. However, the pursuit of an investigation does provide a meaning for the practice of such skills although, at times, the enthusiasm for what is being expressed may hamper the memory of some of the rules of English. Even so, the examples of work given have not always been the final reports, and the prestige of presenting a final report for a class book or for display has often improved the quality of presentation, including that of written English, beyond recognition.

The teacher has been mentioned rather infrequently, not because the role is unimportant but because it is relatively unobtrusive. The demands on the teacher are, however, great, as regards guiding children towards (sometimes away from) further investigations. The teacher needs to be aware of the stimuli likely to provoke a response, and to anticipate (supported by material readiness and some background knowledge) the lines of development which are likely to occur. Fortunately, the teacher's task is eased as children extend and bring to the classroom their interests and hobbies, and when children find that cooperation between individuals is a necessity, rather than something to be deplored.

It is all too easy to point to missed opportunities in the situations concerned. (Wouldn't it have been a good thing if Charlie had been taken to see the coal mining exhibit at the—not too distant—museum?) Undoubtedly, opportunities often were and are missed for many reasons, such as lack of experience on the part of a teacher, large numbers in the class, and so on. However, there is also much more to be learned about the best ways of harnessing the energy which children have available for their interests, and of avoiding excessive teacher involvement which may 'kill' interests.

It should now be possible to look back at the development of the children's work under the following headings.

1. The various starting points for studies, including:
    (a) children's own collections and interests;
    (b) visits to the local environment; walks, exploration, etc;
    (c) the classroom interest table, which is best seen as a selection (made by the teacher and the children) of items from the environment which may be used for further investigation;
    (d) books (including stories, etc);
    (e) audio-visual aids (including television, sound broadcasts, films, etc);
    (f) visits to special parts of the environment such as museums, zoos, etc (the examples given have deliberately been restricted to the more local environment).

2. The need for a variety of material to arouse interests.

3. The importance of opportunities for careful

observations (including handling of material).

4. The various methods by which records may be kept and the relationship of science to work in the basic skills.

5. The importance of discussion both as a method of communication and as a way of clarifying problems.

6. The need actually to perform practical investigations.

Appendix

Classroom resources

Many primary schools have discovered that complex apparatus is not a necessary pre-requisite for scientific studies. Often, pieces of 'equipment' to hand are as satisfactory as their commercial counterparts, as well as being considerably cheaper; for example, transparent plastic containers and glass jars may replace beakers, although admittedly they cannot be heated over a flame. Frequently, materials discarded by an affluent society provide valuable equipment for school use. Collection of such materials may be a major exercise, but children and parents cooperate when given a lead by the teacher. Although storage may present a problem, this can be eased by the fact that many items may be of use in studies other than science, and their lack of any monetary value means that they do not need to be locked away.

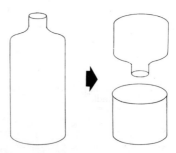

Beaker and funnel made from bottle

The list below represents an attempt to categorize some of the numerous items which may be useful. Many of these things will be found to have a multitude of uses, although some ingenuity may be required to realize their potential. The discovery that a plastic dispensing bottle may be cut in half to make a 'beaker' and 'funnel' has certainly been made independently on many occasions.

Undoubtedly many teachers and children have found uses for the 'nozzle' left over. One such use has been as a pan for a delicate balancing, also using a drinking straw, a pin, and a piece of bent metal strip:

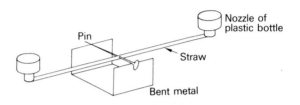

Another use for plastic bottles has been to make water wheels:

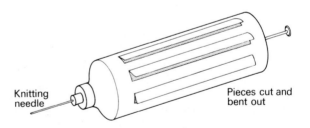

Another use is, combined with a large glass jar, to make a simple wormery. (See the illustration on page 48.)

Worms live in soil in the space between the inside of the glass and the outside of the plastic bottle.

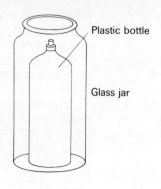

Plastic bottle

Glass jar

And so it may go on; the list of possibilities is almost endless.

Materials **Stationery etc:** paper, cardboard, blotting paper (useful as filter paper), glue, paste, greaseproof paper, tissue paper, adhesive tape, paper clips, drawing pins, pins, staples, string, elastic bands, scissors, ink (red ink is a useful biological stain), old ballpoint pens and packages, powder paint, sealing wax, drinking straws, clay, oil-based clay, plaster of Paris.

Tools etc: hammer, saw, pliers, screwdriver, penknife, screws, nails, washers, sandpaper. (A piece of timber can span desks or tables to make a work bench.)

Containers (usually discarded ones): saucepans, trays, plastic bowls, plastic buckets, containers made of polythene, polystyrene, etc (eg, egg containers, ice trays, ice-cream tubs), polythene storage containers, plastic spray bottles, etc, jam jars and other glass containers (small bottles made to hold food flavouring make useful dropping bottles), metal containers (including those which have held canned food), spoons, plastic bags, cardboard boxes (match boxes are particularly useful).

'Chemicals' (a) *from domestic sources;* common salt (sodium chloride), Epsom salts, baking powder, washing soda, starch, liquid detergent, detergent powder, bleach, water softener, methylated spirits, ammonia, vinegar, sugar, citric acid, talcum powder, food colouring;
(b) *from builders, timber merchants;* sand, cement, fine gravel, lime, asbestos sheet (for heat-resistant bench covers), offcuts of timber and surfacing materials, and *named* timber samples.

Domestic junk (excluding containers): needles, thread, stockings (for making nets, etc), cardboard rolls, metal and other bottle tops, expanded polystyrene packing and ceiling tiles, polyurethane 'sponges', old brushes (especially tooth brushes), sieves and strainers, pieces of candles, metal (wire) clothes hangers, corks, mirrors, clocks, electrical apparatus (beware of television tubes), eye droppers (pipettes).

Material from further afield: old bicycles; for gear wheels, steel tubes, chromium plated steel, rubber tubing, valves, metal spokes, ball bearings, dynamos, lamps, wire, brake levers, saddle springs, etc; old cars; for most of the above and for electric motors, coil, mirrors (plane and convex), pulley wheels, various metals and plastics, switches, speedometers and other instruments, etc.

Also materials from: (a) *plumbers:* piping of different materials such as copper, brass, lead, iron, steel, plastics;
(b) *electricians and telephone engineers:* wire, switches, fuse boxes, connecting boxes, etc;
(c) *opticians:* lenses.

(Many of the items listed above would, of course, not be in the possession of a teacher, but sources of such materials could be discovered.)
Some other equipment might need to be purchased, especially for work at the junior stage.

Simple equipment might include: thermometers, magnets, magnetic compass, corks, plastic tubing, pulleys, spirit lamp, lenses, and a simple microscope.

Booklist

Allen, G. E. et al SCIENTIFIC INTERESTS IN THE PRIMARY
SCHOOL National Froebel Foundation 1960

CHILDREN LEARNING: THROUGH SCIENTIFIC INTEREST
National Froebel Foundation 1966

Isaacs, N. EARLY SCIENTIFIC TRENDS IN CHILDREN
National Froebel Foundation 1958

NATURE ACTIVITIES IN SCHOOLS School Natural Science
Society 1970

Nuffield Junior Science Project: TEACHER'S GUIDE 1;
TEACHER'S GUIDE 2; ANIMALS AND PLANTS; APPARATUS
Collins 1967

SCIENCE AND MATHEMATICS FOR PRIMARY SCHOOLS Essex
County Council Education Committee 1967

Science for Primary Schools: 1. CHILDREN LEARNING
THROUGH SCIENCE; 2. LIST OF BOOKS; 3. LIST OF TEACH-
ING AIDS; 4. MATERIALS AND EQUIPMENT John Murray
(for the Association for Science Education) 1966

THE ESS READER by Elementary Science Study.
Newton: Mass. Education Development Center
1970

Some useful addresses are:

National Froebel Foundation
2 Manchester Square, London W1. Publications are
available from: East Sussex Office Equipment, 204–
206 London Road, East Grinstead, Sussex.

School Natural Science Society
Publications are obtainable from M. J. Wootton,
44 Claremont Gardens, Upminster, Essex RM14 1RS.

Essex County Council Education Committee
Schools Department, County Hall, Chelmsford,
Essex.

See also the following booklets in this series: AN INTRODUCTION, ENVIRONMENTAL STUDIES, MATHEMATICS FOR YOUNGER CHILDREN, MATHEMATICS FOR OLDER CHILDREN, A RURAL SCHOOL, AN INFANT SCHOOL, A JUNIOR SCHOOL, THE TEACHER'S ROLE, and EDUCATING TEACHERS.

Glossary

For a fuller understanding of some terms that are briefly defined in the following list, the reader is referred to one or more books in this series.

Cooperative teaching
Team teaching. An example of cooperative teaching is described in detail in A RURAL SCHOOL.

Eleven plus (11+)
Term used to cover the procedures and techniques (eg, attainment and/or intelligence tests, and teachers' reports) used by local education authorities mainly to select pupils for grammar schools at the age of 11; formerly in universal use, now decreasingly, and only in areas where selection continues. A view of the eleven plus is given in AN INTRODUCTION by Joseph Featherstone.

Family grouping
See **Vertical grouping.**

Grammar school
Academic High School.

Half-term
Mid-semester (see also **Term**).

Hall
Multi-purpose space, large enough to hold the whole school (staff and pupils). Usually a large room, often combining the functions of dining hall, auditorium and gymnasium.

Headteacher
Principal. For an examination of the headteacher's work, and the differences between headteachers and US principals, see THE HEADTEACHER'S ROLE and THE GOVERNMENT OF EDUCATION.

Health visitor
Qualified nurse with special training who is employed by the local education authority to visit schools to check on the children's health.

Her Majesty's Inspector (HMI)
Her Majesty's Inspector of Schools. Appointed formally by the Privy Council to advise the Department of Education and Science, and schools, on the practices and standards of education; and to maintain liaison between the DES and local education authorities. See also THE GOVERNMENT OF EDUCATION.

Infant school	School or department for children from five to seven or eight years old.
Integrated day	A school day in which children may pursue various interests or themes, without regard to artificial divisions into time periods. The workings of an integrated day are fully described in A RURAL SCHOOL.
Junior school	School for seven to eleven or twelve year olds.
Local education authority (LEA)	County or county borough council with responsibility for public education in its area. See THE GOVERNMENT OF EDUCATION.
Movement	An activity where the children explore expressive, agile, and games-like situations. This is done through the dynamic use of the body, with spatial orientation as it comes into contact with people and objects.
Primary school	School for children under twelve. It may be an **Infant school** or **Junior school** (*qq.v.*) or a combination of both.
School managers	Members of an appointed managing body of not fewer than six members who are representative of various interests concerned with the school. For a fuller explanation, and information on the powers and responsibilities of school managers, see THE GOVERNMENT OF EDUCATION.
School year	This begins in September and consists of three terms (see **Terms**).
Special classes	Remedial classes.
Standards I-VIII	Grades in the former Elementary Schools (for children from five to fourteen years).
Streaming	Tracking.
Teachers' centre	A centre set up by a local education authority to provide opportunities for curriculum development and associated in-service training for teachers. See EDUCATING TEACHERS.
Term	The English school year is divided into three terms (cf semesters): Autumn (Fall), Spring, and Summer.
Timetable	Schedule.
Tuition	Teaching. (In Britain, the word 'tuition' never has the meaning, 'fees'.)
Vertical grouping	(also called **Family grouping**): Form of grouping, found mainly in infant schools, in which the full age range for which the school provides may be represented in each class. See also SPACE, TIME AND GROUPING.